TU

CW00401467

TUSCANY & UMBRIA

A Collection of the Poetry of Place

Edited by
GAIA SERVADIO

ELAND • LONDON

First published in October 2011 by Eland Publishing Ltd,
61 Exmouth Market, Clerkenwell, London EC1R 4QL

All poems © of the authors and translators, as attributed
in the text and in the acknowledgements

ISBN 978 1 906011 56 7

Pages designed and typeset by Antony Gray
Cover image: *Landscape* by Orlando Mostyn-Owen,
by kind permission of the artist
Printed and bound in Spain by GraphyCems, Navarra

This book is dedicated to
Maria Fairweather,
who loved Italy

Contents

SENTIMENTAL JOURNEYS OF
LOVE AND HATRED

JOURNEYING THROUGH TUSCAN
AND UMBRIAN CITIES

A JOURNEY OF MEMORIES AND RECOLLECTIONS

A JOURNEY AROUND DANTE AND
THE BEAUTY OF THE TUSCAN LANGUAGE

Foreword

Although the borders of Tuscany and Umbria intertwine and have at times changed,[1] the two regions are separated more by their differences than united by the little they have in common. The Tuscans, as their name betrays, historically were Etruscans; and they border the Tyrrhenian Sea unlike Umbria, which is landlocked. In order to build monuments and cathedrals, the Umbrians could only rely on clay, stone and tufa while, on the other hand, the Tuscans could count on marble and pink travertine. Michelangelo climbed the glittering mountains of the Apuane to choose the rocks he wanted to chisel; Agostino di Duccio – who, although he was Tuscan worked mainly in Umbria – had to use majolica, stone and bricks. The Umbrian poverty stimulated a deep mysticism which exploded with Christianity, producing people such as St Francis of Assisi, Jacopone da Todi and Sister Angela da Foligno – a mad mystic who described her holy masturbations.

The genius of Tuscany shone in the Renaissance while that of Umbria thrived in the Middle Ages. In Tuscany people speak most beautifully while in Umbria the Italian language is murdered. The Tuscans have a guttural edge in their speech that descends from the ancient Etruscans who were people from the east. According to Herodotus the Etruscans – Thirrenii for the Greeks, Tusci for the Latins – had originally come from Anatolia and, as usual, Herodotus was right; the Umbrians instead are indigenous.

Umbrian women were modest, their Tuscan sisters were bold and fair.

---

1 For example, Sansepolcro used to be in Tuscany and now it is within Umbria while Rieti and Orte which were Umbrian are now in Latium.

> Already in my vision is a time to come to which this hour
> Shall not be very old, when the brazen-faced women
> of Florence
> Shall be forbidden from the pulpit to go abroad
> Showing their breasts with their paps.[2]

Thus thunders Dante.

The Tuscans are brilliant traders and fabulous artisans, the Umbrians tend to be withdrawn and take umbrage easily.

After the fall of the Roman Empire, most of Umbria was conquered by the Lombards who added an abstract dimension to the Umbrian sense of aesthetics. At the Abbazia of San Pietro in Valle, in Val Nerina, a Duke of Spoleto (eighth century) was interred in a classical Roman sarcophagus; on the one side, warring Amazons and the usual galloping horses; on the other a Teutonic hand sculpted an image of the cosmos in mysterious, Wagnerian mood.

When Umbria was conquered by Cesare Borgia, the Pope's son, his sister Lucrezia became the Duchess of Spoleto and entered the city covered in gold. All the Umbrian barons had been slaughtered, after accepting an invitation to dine with Cesare, whose name in Umbria is cursed to this day and who is better known as Il Valentino.[3] Today, those who explore Umbrian cuisine do not risk being poisoned, quite the opposite; food in Umbria is simple and delicious. On the other hand the best book of Italian cuisine was written back in the 1920s by the Tuscan Pellegrino Artusi.

When visiting Umbria and Tuscany, poets described a beauty which at times could be wounding and overwhelming but invariably stimulated their imagination; struck by majestic

2 *Purgatorio*, XXIII
3 From Valentinois, a title he received from the French king, which refers to his Valencian origins.

visions or by unsuppressed enthusiasm, they wrote wonderful and melancholic lines.

Beauty can be disturbing; some poets expressed hatred, others ecstasy and, even the English, who are resistant to the impact of emotions (with the overwhelming exception of Lord Byron) seem to have got Florence and Tuscany under their skin. Italian poets glorified the wonders of the region's nature and monuments but the Tuscans! They never forget their land, their women, their Florence.

Dante hated Florence, the city that had exiled him but, at the same time, longed for it; many poetic voices in this anthology blame the city for not having given burial to its greatest poet. Dante also witnessed his world's decline as we are watching ours and he blamed new money, new people and their ignorance just as we do today. 'Rejoice Florence because you are so great that your wings beat over the seas and land and your name echoes about the entire Hell.'[4]

I start with the cinemascopic journey of Childe Harold which embraces both Tuscany and Umbria. In this initial journey through the two regions, Byron visited the Franciscan Basilica of Santa Croce in Florence, the resting place, the Pantheon of those who made the city great, like Boccaccio, Rossini (although he was not a Tuscan and his heart was, in all senses, in Paris) Galileo, Michelangelo, Alberti and Machiavelli amongst others, but notoriously not Dante.

Byron then goes to Lake Trasimene where the Carthaginians clashed with the Romans leaving the memory of a blood bath in the local place names; as well as Sanguinetto (from *sangue*, blood), Cecanibbi is meant to be named after Hannibal was blinded (*cieco Annibale*).

---

4 'Godi Fiorenza perche' sei si grande che per mare e per terra sbatti l'ali e per l'Inferno il tuo nome si spande.' See page 72.

FROM *Childe Harold's Pilgrimage (Canto IV)*
LORD BYRON (1788–1824)

LIX

And Santa Croce wants their mighty dust;
Yet for this want more noted, as of yore
The Caesar's pageant, shorn of Brutus' bust,
Did but of Rome's best son remind her more:
Happier Ravenna! on thy hoary shore,
Fortress of falling empire! Honour'd sleeps
The immortal exile; Arqua, too, her store
Of tuneful relics proudly claims and keeps,
While Florence vainly begs her banish'd dead and weeps.

LXII

       . . . and I roam
By Thrasimene lakes, in the defiles
Fatal to Roman rashness, more at home;
For there the Carthagenian's warlike wiles
Come back before me, as his skill beguiles
The host between the mountains and the shore,
Where Courage falls in her despairing files,
And torrents, swoln to rivers with their gore,
Reek through the sultry plain, with legions scatter'd o'er.

LXIII

Like to a forest fell'd by mountain winds;
And such the storm of battle on this day,

And such the frenzy, whose convulsion blinds
To all save carnage, that, beneath the fray,
An earthquake reel'd unheededly away!
None felt stern nature rocking at his feet,
And yawning forth a grave for those who lay
Upon their bucklers for a winding sheet;
Such is the absorbing hate when warring nations meet!

LXIV

The earth to them was as a rolling bark
Which bore them to Eternity; they saw
The ocean round, but had no time to mark
The motions of their vessel; nature's law,
In them suspended, reck'd not of the awe
Which reigns when mountains tremble, and the birds
Plunge in the clouds for refuge and withdraw
From their down-toppling nests; and bellowing herds
Stumble o'er heaving plains, and man's dread hath no words.

LXV

Far other scene is Thrasimene now;
Her lake a sheet of silver, and her plain
Rent by no ravage save the gentle plough;
Her aged trees rise thick as once the slain
Lay where their roots are; but a brook hath ta'en –
A little rill of scanty stream and bed –
A name of blood from that day's sanguine rain;
And Sanguinetto tells ye where the dead
Made the earth wet. And turn'd the unwilling waters red.

Introduction

According to Laurence Sterne, those who ventured abroad, poets as well as ordinary travellers, were driven by 'one of these general causes:

> Infirmity of mind,
> Imbecility of mind,
> Inevitable necessity.'

He added that there were other categories of travellers, such as

> 'the Idle Travellers,
> the Inquisitive Travellers,
> the Lying Travellers,
> the Proud Travellers,
> the Vain Travellers,
> the Splenetic Travellers,
> The Travellers of necessity . . .

and last of all (if you please)

> The Sentimental Travellers

(meaning thereby myself) . . . '

A Sentimental Traveller is a Traveller of Poetry, fortunate because he can travel with his mind thus avoiding the hassle and discomfort of airports, delays and disappointments. The traveller of poetry is melancholic and treasures memories of holding hands with a beloved under a restaurant table, kissing at a café, walking together along a country lane on the wings of poetry.

> Tunc amo, tunc odi frusta, quod amare necessite est
> Tunc ego, sed tecum mortuus esse velim.[5]

---

5 'Then I love you, then I hate you; in vain because I need to love you. And then I would like to die, but with you.' Ovid

Travelling in the mind's eye, that is, with poetry, is cheaper than taking a plane and hiring a car and often more rewarding. One avoids noting how much cement has spoiled one's favourite landscape; how many objects have been stolen from a beloved museum or how those that you had come especially to see are travelling themselves to exhibitions in Tokyo or Cincinnati.

But of course, every day is a journey, we wake in the morning and we travel through the day, each day a different voyage. At times our night turns into a canvas for our journeys, which we remember in the morning for a short time, and then forget, like a line of poetry.

I once returned to the temple of Clitumnus near Trevi, in Umbria, which was a holy spot described in this anthology by Virgil, Byron, d'Annunzio and Carducci. My father used to take me there, and his enthusiasm for the perfect little temple and the immaculate water that mirrored the elegance of the Doric capitols reached poetry. In his company I myself saw nymphs and the very god Clitumnus, dripping watery flowers and surrounded by fauns. The pond was a Claude landscape, a song by Monteverdi in itself. Then my father died and so did Clitumnus. A barrier of cement has been allowed to bar the perfect architecture that centuries had respected – and praised.

Preserved by centuries of poverty, other parts of Umbria were also destroyed by local councils, overwhelmed by too much money, ignorance, corruption and power. To visit would be a journey of rage, which I prefer to avoid. So I return to a poetic Sentimental Journey.

In October 1786 Goethe was in Perugia and sat down to write his diary of the previous few days; he loved Tuscany and observing the culture of vines and olive groves, wrote that he had never seen 'a better kept countryside than around Arezzo.'

When his coach stopped at Assisi, he left it and climbed the windswept hill, in order to see the temple dedicated to Minerva,[6] not Giotto's (1266–1337) or Cimabue's (before 1231–1302) frescoes (he was only interested in Classicism).[7]

6 J. Wolfgang Goethe, *Travels in Italy*
7 Dante praises the greatness of Giotto who overtook his *maestro* Cimabue.

> 'Credette Cimabue nella pittura
> tener lo campo, e ora ha Giotto il grido,
> sì che la fama di colui oscura.'

> 'Once Cimabue thought to hold the field
> of painting; Giotto now is all the rage,
> dimming the lustre of the other's fame.'

JOURNEY THROUGH THE LANDSCAPE

The Tuscan Landscape

DANTE ALIGHIERI (1265–1321)

from *The Divine Comedy*
The Inferno, Canto XXX
Translated by Alistair Elliot

The little brooks which down from the green hills
of Casentino splash towards the Arno,
making their channels smooth and soft and chill,
hang always here before me – not in vain:
for the image of them desiccates me more
than this disease, which sucks my face so thin.

Clitumnus and the Waterfall at Marmore

LORD BYRON (1788–1824)

from *Childe Harold's Pilgrimage (Canto IV)*

LXVI

But thou, Clitumnus! in thy sweetest wave
Of the most living crystal that was e'er
The haunt of river nymph, to gaze and lave
Her limbs where nothing hid them, thou dost rear
Thy grassy banks whereon the milk-white steer
Grazes; the purest god of gentle waters!
And most serene of aspect, and most clear;
Surely that stream was unprophaned by slaughters –
A mirror and a bath for Beauty's youngest daughters!

LXVII

And on thy happy shore a temple still,
Of small and delicate proportion, keeps,
Upon a mild declivity of hill,
Its memory of thee; beneath it sweeps
Thy current's calmness; oft from out it leaps
The finny darter with the glittering scales,
Who dwells and revels in thy glassy deeps;
While, chance, some scatter'd water-lily sails
Down where the shallower wave still tells its bubbling tales.

LXIX

The roar of waters! – from the headlong height
Velino cleaves the wave-worn precipice;

The fall of waters! rapid as the light
The flashing mass foams shaking the abyss;
The hell of waters! where they howl and hiss,
And boil in endless torture; while the sweat
Of their great agony, wrung out from this
Their Phlegethon, curls round the rocks of jet
That gird the gulf around, in pitiless horror set,

LXX

And mounts in spray the skies, and thence again
Returns in an unceasing shower, which round,
With its unemptied cloud of gentle rain,
Is an eternal April to the ground,
Making it all one emerald: how profound
The gulf! and how the giant element
From rock to rock leaps with delirious bound,
Crushing the cliffs, which, downward worn and rent
With his fierce footsteps, yield in chasms a fearful vent.

Here Byron describes the magic peace of the temple holy to
Clitumnus, near Trevi. And he goes to see the majestic waterfalls
of Le Marmore, in Val Nerina, whose tumbling foam reaches us
through the poetry.

The Source of the God Clitumnus

VIRGIL (70–19BC)

from the *Georgics*
Translated by Gualtiero Maldè

. . . happy land of herds and olive groves.
The warhorses stand here, powerful on the field;
From here, oh Clitumnus! the flock of dazzling white
                                          sheep and the bull,
magnificent victim, dripping from your sacred river,
lead to the sacrificial temple in expectation of Roman triumphs.
Here is the long-lasting Spring
and the extended Summer sunsets; and trees and buds,
and branches heavy with apples, and fecund animals.
Not here angry tigers and cruel lions;
Nor this grass, mingled with poisons, cheats miserable gatherers
And scaly snakes do not slide on the grass with huge bulges
Nor do they stand in coils writhing from the ground.

. . . (the plough) will give rich vines and rich
with Bacchus' juice this land is fertile with grapes, with wine
that we drink in golden cups when the stalwart Etruscan
has blown the flute near the altars
and we offer steaming entrails in large dishes.

. . . enent oleae armentaque laeta.
Hinc bellator equos campo sese arduus infert,
hinc albi, clitumne, greges et maxima Taurus
victima saepe tuo perfusi flumine sacro
Romanos ad templa deum duxere triumphos.
Hic ver adsiduum atque alienis mensibus aestas;
Bis graviudae tigres absunt et saeva leonum
Semina, nec miseros fallunt aconirta legentis,
Nec rapiut immensos orbis per humum neque tanto
Squameus in spiram tractu se colligit anguis.

…hic tibi praevalidas olim multoque fluentis
sufficiet Baccho vitis, hic fertilis uvae,
hic laticis, qualem pateris libamus et auro,
inflavit cum pinguis ebur Tyrrhenus ad aras
lancibus et pandas fumantia reddimus extra.

From *At the Springs of the Clitumnus*

GIOSUÈ CARDUCCI (1835–1907)

Translated by Alistair Elliot

Even today from the hill, whose back ripples
with dim ash trees muttering in the wind and
spreads far on the breeze wafts of its own fresh smell
of wild sage and thyme,

the flocks come down through moistening air at sunset
to you, Clitumnus; still the Umbrian boy
plunges his struggling animal under your
ruffled surface, while

to see him from the breast of their tanned mother
who sits barefoot beside the shieling and sings,
his small unweaned sister pushes round and sends
a full round-faced smile;

there still the anxious father, with his thighs wrapped
in hairy goatskins like the fauns long ago,
rules and directs his painted cart and the strength
of his fine oxen,

those lovely oxen with their square honest chests,
and crescent horns set high above their foreheads,
and great soft eyes, the snowy beasts that tender
Virgil was fond of.

Carducci spent most of his life teaching; my generation knew by heart *I Cipressi che a Bolgheri alti e stretti*, a poem that gave the name to the needle-like cypresses which are so fashionable today with second-house owners but are less pleasing for birds which cannot build nests within their slight frames. Carducci, a classicist, spent his childhood at Bolgheri, near Florence. The son of a revolutionary, a very erudite man, a classicist, he enjoyed enormous fame in Italy and France.

Angels in Italy, Garfagnana

AL ALVAREZ (1929–)

They make no noise, though their wings move,
Pale white against pale blue; upwards and slow,
Watching us, curious, clear eyes, clear foreheads,
Hair streaming away behind, sun in sun,
Till the flank of the mountain hides them,
Chestnut, spruce, scrub oak and fir
Tangling up to the ridge. Then blue, blue, blue.

Such solitude. Calm faces, falling hair,
Poised wings and sinewy pinions. The clouds
Have them now. Soaring, circling. Gone away.
Leaving the murmur of water, vine leaves saying, 'Shush,'
Leaves of the walnut rattling like dice.

A car rasps in the valley. Someone is cutting
Wood with a buzz-saw, harsh, not letting go.
Now come the children, the wives, the gossip and cooking,
Evening and thickening light. A brisk wind sweeps
From ridge to ridge bringing silence.
Each of us pauses, absent, lost in himself,
Stilled by the sound of the river.

A glint of white against blue.
'Clouds', you say, 'clouds.'
No, wings. Listen. Wings heavily beating,
Rustle of feathers, shoulders flexing smoothly
Beyond the ridge. But I answer,
'Clouds, yes, clouds.
Tomorrow, love, tomorrow there'll be rain.'

La Garfagnana, an extremely beautiful area between Lucca and the Apuan Alps, has been a land of poets; for a time its governor was Ludovico Ariosto. Al Alvarez has a house in the Garfagnana although I don't know how many angels lived in it.

Evening: Ponte al Mare, Pisa

PERCY BYSSHE SHELLEY (1792–1822)

I

The sun is set; the swallows are asleep;
The bats are flitting fast in the grey air;
The slow soft toads out of damp corners creep,
And evening's breath, wandering here and there
Over the quivering surface of the stream,
Wakes not one ripple from its summer dream.

II

There is no dew on the dry grass tonight,
Nor damp within the shadow of the trees;
The wind is intermitting, dry, and light;
And in the inconstant motion of the breeze
The dust and straws are driven up and down,
And whirled about the pavement of the town.

III

Within the surface of the fleeting river
The wrinkled image of the city lay,
Immovably unquiet, and forever
It trembles, but it never fades away;
Go to thee …
You, being changed, will find it then as now.

IV

The chasm in which the sun has sunk is shut
By darkest barriers of cinereous cloud,
Like mountain over mountain huddled – but
Growing and moving upwards in a crowd,
And over it a space of watery blue
Which the keen evening star is shining through.

Shelley, who drowned off Tuscany in 1822, lived in Lerici for a while, in a little house which we, my sister and I, as children, used to pass on our way to the Golfo dei Poeti.

News from Mount Amiata

EUGENIO MONTALE (1896–1981)

'Imitated' by Robert Lowell

I

Come night,
the ugly weather's fire-cracker simmer
will deepen to the gruff buzz of beehives.
Termites tunnel the public room's rafters to sawdust,
an odour of bruised melons oozes from the floor.
A sick smoke lifts from the elf huts and funghi of the valley –
like an eagle it climbs our mountain's bald cone,
and soils the windows,
and I write to you –
here on this mountain, in this beehive cell
on the globe rocketed through space.
My letter is a paper hoop.
When I break through it, you will be imprisoned.

Here mildew sprouts like grass from the floor,
the canary cage is hooded with dirty green serge,
chestnuts explode on the grate.
Outside, it's raining.
There you are legendary.
Any legend falls short, if it confine you,
your gold-gated icon unfolding on gold.

II

Magnesium flares light up the hidden summits;
but the narrow feudal streets below are too dark
for the caravan of black donkeys kicking up sparks.

You are devoted to precarious
sentiments and sediments-blackened architecture;
rectangular courtyards centred
on bottomless wells. You are led
by the sinister wings of nightbirds,
the infinite pit, the luminous gape of the galaxies –
all their sleight of hand and torture.
But the step that carries out into darkness
comes from a man going alone,
who sees nothing but the nearest light-chinked shutter,
The stars' pattern is too deep for him,
atmospheric ivy only chokes his darkness,
his campanile shuts its eyes at two o'clock.

III

Here on this mountain,
the world has no custom-barriers.
Let tomorrow be colder, let the north wind
shatter the stringy ribbons of old Missals,
the sandstone bastion of the barbarians.
When our sensations have no self-assurance,
everything must be a lens.
Then the polar winds will return clearer,
and convert us to our chains, the chains of the possible.

IV

Today, the monotonous oratory of the dead,
ashes, lethargic winds –
a reluctant trickle drips
from the thatched huts.
Time is water.
The rain rains down black letters –
a *contemptu mundi!* What part of me does it bring you?

Now at this late hour
of my watch and your endless, prodigal sleep,
my tiny straw city is breaking up.
The porcupine sips a quill of mercy.

Montale, who won the Nobel Prize in Literature in 1975, is Italy's outstanding poet of the twentieth century. He translated Eliot and suffered for his antifascism. Lowell, the Bostonian poet whose elegance of verse in a way echoes Montale's, was a great admirer of his.

Mont'Amiata, a volcanic mountain near Seggiano in Tuscany, is scattered with wonderful monasteries, some of which are famous for their Gregorian chanting.

MYSTICAL JOURNEYS

The first poems in this section owe their origins to Umbria's distinctive role in the history of early Christian mysticism: it is both the birthplace of the founder of the first monastic order, and of St Francis who went on to found another.

The quintessential Umbrian mystic, and one of its most famous sons, is St Francis of Assisi, the son of a merchant, born in 1182, who gave everything away and, at the age of twenty-four, founded the Order of the Franciscans which contrasted with the papacy so much that St Francis risked being burnt alive. The Curia regarded him as a heretic.

The very first monastic order was founded by an Umbrian, St Benedict (sixth century). And Jacopone da Todi (1230–1306), a Benedictine monk, wrote in the same mystical, simple mood as St Francis. His famous poem 'Stabat Mater', set to music by Rossini, Pergolesi, Scarlatti, Palestrina, Vivaldi and Dvorjak amongst others, was written in the Medieval Latin that is almost Italian (as indeed St Francis' Italian is almost Latin).

Canticle of All Creatures

FRANCIS OF ASSISI (1181/2–1226)

Most high, all powerful, good Lord!
All praise is yours, all glory, and also all honour, and all blessing.
To you, alone, Most High, do they belong.
No one is worthy to pronounce your name.
Be praised, my Lord, through all your creatures,
especially through Brother Sun, who brings the day;
and you give light through him.
And he is beautiful and radiant in all his splendour!
Of you, Most High, he bears the likeness.
Be praised, my Lord, through Sister Moon and the stars;
in the heavens you shaped them bright, precious and beautiful.
Be praised, my Lord, through Brother Wind and Air,
and clouds and storms, and all the seasons,
through which you give your creatures sustenance.
Be praised, My Lord, through Sister Water;
she is very useful, and humble, and precious, and pure.
Be praised, my Lord, through Brother Fire,
through whom you brighten the night.
He is beautiful and cheerful, and powerful and strong.
Be praised, my Lord, through our sister Mother Earth,
who feeds and rules us,
and produces various fruits with coloured flowers and herbs.
Be praised, my Lord, through those who forgive for love of you;
through those who endure sickness and trial.
Happy those who endure in peace,
for by you, Most High, they will be crowned.
Be praised, my Lord, through our Sister Bodily Death,

from which no living person can escape.
Woe to those who die in mortal sin!
Happy those she finds doing your most holy will.
Because the second death will not harm them.
Praise and bless my Lord, and give thanks,
and serve him with great humility.

The Laurel Tree

GABRIELE D'ANNUNZIO (1863–1938)

Translated by Gualtiero Maldè

In the orchard, at Massa – Oh! azure blocks,
Alps Apuane! Hazy turquoise sculpture
In the bluish air, at the brim of the city!

A scented and shiny orchard
Full of tremulous whispers
Dense with birds' music.

Inside the courtyard, the magnolia
Springs its dense scent; at dawn
I stood at the foot of a slender laurel tree.

Stabat Mater

JACOPONE DA TODI (1230–1306)

Stabat mater dolorosa
juxta Crucem lacrimosa
dum pendebat Filius.

Cuius animam gementem,
contristatam et dolentem
pertransivit gladius.

O quam tristis et afflicta
fuit illa benedicta
mater Unigeniti!

Quae moerebat et dolebat
pia Mater, dum videbat
nati poenas incliti.

Quis est homo qui non fleret,
matrem Christi si videret
in tanto supplicio?

At the Cross her station keeping,
stood the mournful Mother weeping,
close to her Son to the last.

Through her heart, His sorrow sharing,
all His bitter anguish bearing
now at length the sword had passed.

O how sad and sore distressed
was that Mother, highly blest,
of the sole-begotten One.

Christ above in torment hangs,
she beneath beholds the pangs
of her dying glorious Son.

Is there one who would not weep,
Whelmed in miseries so deep,
Chrsist's dear mother to behold?

The translation of this – longer, much longer – and famous
poem is not literal but is rendered in words which are close to
the original tempo.

The Abbey of Vallombrosa in the Apennines

ALPHONSE DE LAMARTINE (1790–1869)

Translated by Gualtiero Maldè

Human spirit, a day over these icy summits,
Far from an odious world, which gust brought you here?
You were, right to the summit, pursued by your thoughts;
What beauty or what horror at last stopped you?

Was it the appeal of those forests, the darkness, that feeling
And those ageless trees, and those immortal rocks,
And that sacred instinct that looks for a new world
Far from the beaten tracks that trick us mortals.

You were not alone there: under divine shapes
Your apparitions crowded those fine places;
You saw, one by one, pass by those hills
The essence of the tempest and God's breath.

Without doubt they taught you that sublime language
That nature inspires in the heart of the desperate;
You understood the winds, the thunder and the tempest,
As elements talk among themselves.

The spirit of prayer and of solitude
Which glides over the mountains, the torrents and the woods,
Which to mortal eyes seems nature at its most rough
Always appealed to select human souls . . .

Esprit de l'homme, un jour sur ces cimes glacées,
Loin d'un monde odieux, quel souffle t'emporta ?
Tu fus jusqu'au sommet chassé par tes pensées ;
Quel charme ou quelle horreur à la fin t'arrêta ?

Ce furent ces forêts, ces ténèbres, cette onde,
Et ces arbres sans date, et ces rocs immortels,
Et cet instinct sacré qui cherche un nouveau monde
Loin des sentiers battus que foulent les mortels.

Tu n'y vécus pas seul : sous des formes divines,
Tes apparitions peuplèrent ce beau lieu ;
Tu voyais tour à tour passer sur ces collines
L'esprit de la tempête et le souffle de Dieu.

Sans doute ils t'enseignaient ce sublime langage
Que parle la nature au cœur des malheureux ;
Tu comprenais les vents, le tonnerre et l'orage,
Comme les éléments se comprennent entre eux.

L'esprit de la prière et de la solitude,
Qui plane sur les monts, les torrents et les bois,
Dans ce qu'aux yeux mortels la terre a de plus rude
Appela de tout temps des âmes de son choix.

Because of a reference to Vallombrosa in Milton's *Paradise Lost*, the Abbey was visited over the years by many. South-east of Florence in the Apennine Mountains, it was founded in the eleventh century as a Benedictine monastery.

A JOURNEY THROUGH ARTISTS AND POLITICS

Those artists who were invited to work for the Holy See in Rome during the Renaissance, when the Pope became the main source of commissions, invariably travelled through Umbria, the coast being too dangerous because of malaria and piracy. Tuscany's greatest talents – Luca Signorelli, Michelangelo, Filippo Lippi and Beato Angelico – all passed though Umbria, a fact which contributed to the greatness of the Umbrian school of painting. Indeed in an area of about thirty square kilometres, straddling Tuscany and Umbria, Michelangelo, Leonardo da Vinci and Piero della Francesca were all born; not a coincidence.

For centuries Umbria belonged to the Papacy and was ruled by a succession of priestly bureaucrats; it still suffers from its historic reverence for bureaucracy. Indeed both regions were considered the heartland of the Communist party – Italia rossa, 'Italy's red heart'. Recently, with the berluscalisation of Italy, even Tuscany and Umbria wavered, with the once left-wing Orvieto falling to a Centre-Right Mayor, but a *simpatico* one.

JOHN MILTON (1608–74)

He [Beelzebub] scarce had ceased when the superior fiend
Was moving toward the shore. His ponderous shield
Ethereal temper, massy, large and round,
Behind him cast. The broad circumference
Hung on his shoulders like the moon whose orb
Through optic glass the Tuscan artist views
At evening from the top of Fesole,
Or in Valdarno to descry new lands,
Rivers, or mountains, in her spotty globe.

The Tuscan artist is Galileo; his country house was situated in Valdarno.

Montefalco

GABRIELE D'ANNUNZIO (1863–1938)

Translated by Gaia Servadio

Montefalco.
You were frescoed by Benozzo,
When young, he moved within your great fine walls
Enamoured of all live creatures
Brother of the Sun, like Francis was.

His painting was as sweet as the apple and the peach trees
On the hillside, and clean like the Clitumnus down
                                    on the plain,
His painting was of flowers and water,
Smiling with St Francis' smile.

And did you not give that colour blue
To your Etruscan, and the green? Green slender branches,
Blue of the hills, homage for the altars;

So that it looks as if the very sky lights
Your countryside and in your deep heart
your soul is beautified by your brushes.

Lucca

GABRIELE D'ANNUNZIO (1863–1938)

Translated by Gaia Servadio

From far away you see the grey olive groves
That in haze confuse the hillside, O Serchio,
And the city surrounded by trees
Where Giunigi's woman is asleep.

Now she sleeps, the flower of marble
Enveloped in materials, lying
on her beautiful sepulchre; and perhaps once
You mirrored her; once your bank knew her steps.

But today it is not Ilaria del Carretto
Who commands the land on which you sweep
O Serchio.

These two poems (and others quoted later) are from a collection
of the poetry of Gabriele d'Annunzio called *The Cities of Silence*
(*Le Città del Silenzio*), cities where, the poet implies, nothing
happens any longer.

Benozzo Gozzoli, who signed some of his works *Opus Benozzi
de Florentia*, worked at Montefalco in Umbria on his way to
Rome. In the Montefalco fresco he painted depictions of Dante,
Petrarch and Giotto.

Those who travel to Lucca and visit the sepulchre of Ilaria del
Carretto cannot but be moved by the beauty of the young
woman; Italian girls used to kiss her in the hope that the white
marble would give them some of its glow. It was sculpted by the
Tuscan Jacopo della Quercia (*c.*1374–1438).

Cesare Borgia

NICCOLÒ MACHIAVELLI (1469–1527)

You saw how Pistoia rebelled, in part,
And Florence was full of confusion
You did not have Pisa and Valdichiana

. . .

and he mostly defeated Pistoia
and took back Arezzo and the whole of Valdichiana
under the ancient order.

In Orvieto's cathedral, the chapel frescoed by Signorelli was visited by Michelangelo on his way to Rome. The young Antichrist depicted by Signorelli, a man surrounded by devils, with an icy stare, represented the ambitious Cesare Borgia. Michelangelo remembered the Signorelli's chapel for his Last Judgement. In the Sistine Chapel he depicted his critic, the Pope's Master of Ceremonies, Biagio da Cesena, as Minos, the judge of the Underworld, with donkey's ears.

The chapel was finally completed when Pope Alexander VI, Cesare's father, died in 1503; it was the end of the Borgia family and Central Italy sighed with relief. Indeed the magnificent Santa Maria della Consolazione in Todi, a miracle of Renaissance architecture, was built to express the relief at the consolation of the Borgia pope's death.

. . . Pistoia in parte rebellar vedevi,
e di confusion Firenze pregna
Pisa e Valdichiana non tenevi

. . .

costui Pistoia in gran parte ridusse
costui a Arezzo e tutta Valdichiana
sotto l'antico iugo ricondusse.

Niccolò Machiavelli felt otherwise about the Borgias; he dedicated a poem to the political might of Cesare Borgia, known as 'il Valentino' because he was made Prince of Valentinois by the French king.

This extract is part of a much longer poem from the *Decennale* (1504) written by Niccolò Machiavelli to 'justify' his patron Cesare Borgia.

The Beacons

CHARLES BAUDELAIRE (1821–67)

Translated by Gaia Servadio

...

Leonardo da Vinci, deep and dark mirror
whose charming angels smiling sweetly
appear in the shade, heavy with mystery
of glaciers and pinewoods that frame the view.

...

Michelangelo who mingles Hercules with Christ
in a strange fantasy where powerful ghosts
stand high in the twilight
ripping their shrouds with their horny hands.

These stanzas are taken from a longer poem that encapsulates, verse by brilliant verse, the particular skills of the beacon-like artists who occupy the heights of art history.

FROM *Childe Harold's Pilgrimage*
LORD BYRON (1788–1824)

LIV

In Santa Croce's holy precincts lie
Ashes which make it holier, dust which is
Even in itself an immortality,
Though there were nothing save the past, and this,
The particle of those sublimities
Which have relaps'd to chaos; here repose
Angelo's, Alfieri's bones, and his,
The starry Galileo, with his woes;
Here Machiavelli's earth, return'd to whence it rose.

LV

These are four minds, which, like the elements,
Might furnish forth creation: Italy!
Time, which hath wrong'd thee with ten thousand rents
Of thine imperial garment, shall deny,
And hath denied, to every other sky,
Spirits which soar from ruin: thy decay
Is still impregnate with divinity,
Which guilds it with revivifying ray;
Such as the great of yore, Canova is to-day.

LVI

But where repose the all Etruscan three –
Dante, and Petrarch, and, scarce less than they,

The Bard of Prose, creative spirit! he
Of the Hundred Tales of love – where did they lay
Their bones, distinguish'd from our common clay
In death as life? Are they resolv'd to dust,
And have their country's marbles nought to say?
Could not her quarries furnish forth one bust?
Did they not to her breast their filial earth entrust?

This section of 'Childe Harold's Pilgrimage' finds Byron in the Basilica of Santa Croce in Florence where notable Florentines, and Italians from elsewhere, were buried. Amongst them were Michelangelo, Vittorio Alfieri, an eighteenth-century poet and dramatist, Galileo and Machiavelli. The Bard of Prose refers to Giovanni Boccaccio (1313–75) who was also Tuscan.

Pistoia

GABRIELE D'ANNUNZIO (1863–1938)

Translated by Gaia Servadio

I love you, city of quarrels, angry Pistoia
For the blood of your Bianchi and your Neri
That turns red over your fierce palaces
I see a man of politics of ancient glory.

...

Pistoia in the sacristy full of beautiful robes
I know a more divine smile
Fear, O Pistoia, when the morning
glories over the hills and you don't see it.

From medieval times, Tuscany was politically divided between two factions, the Guelfs and Ghibellines, a division which can still be felt in Italy. The Ghibellines strived for a united Italy under the rule of the Holy Roman Emperor, their name referring to a Swabian castle from which one of their early leaders hailed. The Guelfs, on the other hand, strived to unify Italy under the papacy. In the eighteenth century the Guelfs, then ruling Florence, fought each other as the factions of i Bianchi and i Neri.

As I said, the political division still stands. The Communist party used to rule in the territory of the Ghibellines until Berlinguer confused the Holy See with Brezhnev, so that the modern Guelfs, first embodied by the Christian Democrats and nowadays by their heirs, have won the field.

Orvieto

GAIA SERVADIO

A sharp Gothic star, in Turner, over the city glitters
Over the hills and walls dripping with caper flowers
Violet and white, heart-shaped leaves,
The wooded valleys, the sharp cliffs;
This is a Gothic star
Watching over the drooping cliffs
that shelter sources of water,
Etruscan tombs and walls.
The Lombard towers flank the aqueduct
that brought water from volcanic lakes.
Like a hawk, Turner's brush alights
with the wings of the imagination
Stopping over the cathedral, a façade
Encrusted with choruses of marbles
That tell the story of the elected souls
and of eternal death,
coffins and dancing skeletons play the spectacle
of skill and beauty, on that majestic front.
Turner, the painter, lights the white cathedral.

Sitting at the café,
contemplating Orvieto's sheet of masterpieces
an English youth said, 'I don't like it.'
His eyes were stained and he was stranded
By noisy music and heavy drugs and fear.
Perhaps I did not want to know
what angered his ignorance.

Perhaps he was just stupid.
The falcon shat over his ice cream
Then the noble hawk turned its flight in dust
and channelled its flight indoors,
well inside the white cathedral
where Michelangelo stared at Signorelli's miracle
and watched the Antichrist
smile under a stare of poison.
And flew over the church where the English king's
                                                    brother
Was stabbed.
What did that crusader Prince think
As the knife broke his skin between his royal ribs?
Shakespeare's Hamlet would not have killed
the crusader, praying.
Were his eyes closed by blood?
Perhaps I did not want to know
what angered his ignorance.

Turner, the greatest English painter (1775–1851), was amazed
by the spectacular views of the peaks of the Valle d'Aosta and,
when he saw Orvieto's cathedral, he rendered it like a peak in
the Alps, the cathedral's gothic shape turning into icicles, a
mystical experience in itself. The façade of the cathedral, which
took three centuries to complete, is a compendium of Medieval
Italian sculpture, a jewel.

SENTIMENTAL JOURNEYS OF
LOVE AND HATRED

Ballatetta in Toscana

GUIDO CALVACANTI (*c.*1250–1300)

Translated by Gaia Servadio

Since I do not hope to go back ever
To Tuscany, little Song! fly light and sweet
Go straight to my woman
Who, courteous as she is,
Will honour you.
You will carry sad news
Full of pain and fear;
But watch it, Song, that no one should see you
It might be an enemy with a gentle nature.
It would be my misadventure
Were you to be robbed,
Taken from her, it would pain me;
After my death,
Tears and renewed sorrow.

You know, Little Song, that death
creeps around me so that life abandons me.
Feel how my heart beats strong beats
for the thought of each soul.
My body is already destroyed
for I am unable to suffer
but if you want to serve me, please
take my soul with you.
When it leaves my heart,
I do beg you to do so.

Please, Ballatetta, for our friendship's sake
This trembling soul I entrust.
Take it with you, kind as you are,
To that beautiful woman to whom I am sending you.
Please, Ballatetta, tell her with a sigh
When you are with her:
This servant of yours
Is here to stay by you,
Having taken leave
Of the body which was your servant of love.

You, amazing and weak voice
Emerging from my pain stricken heart,
With my soul and this Ballatetta,
Reason with her about my destroyed mind.

You will find a fine looking woman
Of such sweet intellect
That to be with her
Will delight you always,
Soul, and you will adore her
Always, for her own sake.

Missing his native Tuscany, Guido Cavalcanti, a friend of
Dante's,[8] sends a little song – a Ballatetta – to his beloved,
announcing his own death and, at the same time, the arrival of
his – the poet's – soul.

8 In a sonnet, Dante celebrated their friendship 'Guido vorrei che tu e
   Lapo ed io fossimo presi per incantamento . . . ' Guido, I would like
   that you and Lapo and I were to be swept by magic and swept in a
   vessel . . .

> Perch'io non spero di tornar giammai,
> Ballatetta, in Toscana,
> Va tu, leggera e piana
> Dritt'a la donna mia…

In Guido's poem, la Ballatetta, the little song, becomes an entity, a person, a flying imp.

Love

LORENZO DE' MEDICI (1449–92)

Translated by Ted Hughes

Less and less fearful, more and more beautiful,
Love revealed my adored enemy –
As the thoughts of the day and weariness
Sank into a lazy drowse in the evening.

Shown to my eyes exactly as she is
Only without her usual hard manners,
And wide open to all the loving rays –
Never had any truth seemed so truthful.

Fearful and slow, before I spoke,
I was as I always am. Till dread
Overcame desire, and I began:

'My lady'. – and at that, like a wind, she was gone.
In the same instant she snatched from me
My sleep, herself and my very soul, as she fled.

A Woman Abandoned

LORENZO DE' MEDICI (1449–92)

Translated by Ted Hughes

As if to have taken my freedom were not enough,
And to have wrenched me from my chaste path
Without yet wanting my death,
In such pain and so new to my life,

You left me without a thought.
And when you left me, strengthless and pale
(A true sign that my end would be early)
I remained, hating my own beauty.
Nor can I think of anything but those times
That were the cause of my soft weeping,
My sweet martyrdom, my sad contentment.

If the remembrance were not still one means
Of consoling tortured lovers
I would have ended all this grief by death.

These two love sonnets are by Lorenzo il Magnifico, whose reign
over the Florentine Republic marked the high point of the early
Italian Renaissance.

A Tuscan Love

PETRARCH (1304–74)

Translated by Gaia Servadio and Marcello Simonetta

Ben sapev'io che natural consiglio,
Amor, contra di te gia' mai non valse;
Tanti lacciuol, tante impromesse false,
Tanto provato avea 'l tuo fiero artiglio.
Ma novamente, ond'io mi meraviglio
(Diro''l , come persona a cui ne calse
e che'l notai la' sopra l'acque salse
tra la riva Toscana e l'Elba e Giglio),
'l fuggia le tue mani, e per camino,
agitandom' i venti e 'l cielo e l'onde,
m'andava sconosciuto e pelegrino:
quando ecco i tuoi ministri (i' non so donde)
per darmi a diveder ch'al suo destino
mal chi contrasta e mal chi si nasconde.

Francesco Petrarch met the aging Dante Alighieri when he was a
young boy. Dante must have seemed ageless, forever an adult,
forever angry and an uncomfortable genius. I wonder whether
the young poet understood the importance of that meeting
(Dante had come to see Petrarch's father, also an exile),
although the two poets had such different vocations, Dante
being Michelangelo to Petrarch's Benozzo Gozzoli.
Goethe loved Petrarch, who influenced the whole of Europe and

I knew all too well that one cannot
Fight against you, Love; it never works.
So many snares, so many false promises
your fierce claws made a victim of me.
But again, I am amazed,
(I shall say – as a caring individual –
aware, looking at the sea
between the Tuscan shore
and the islands of Elba and Giglio)
that I escaped from your hands and, as I walked,
while the wind and the sky and the waves
overwhelmed me
there I was, unknown and a pilgrim,
when, here are your ministers! (I know not whence,)
to make me aware that whoever fights
or hides from his destiny, fails Love.

was seen as the embodiment of the revival of the Middle Ages. In his sonnet, 'The Epochs', he wrote: 'Good Friday was engraved in letters of fire at the bottom of Petrarca's heart, more than any other day.' This referred to the story of Petrarch's unrequited love for a woman, Laura, whom he first espied on Good Friday, and about whom he went on to write a collection of influential poems. This offering, however, is inspired by another woman.

Hatred of Pisa

DANTE ALIGHIERI (1265–1321)

from *The Inferno*

Translated by Robert Pinsky

Ah Pisa! You shame the peoples of the fair land
Where *si* is spoken: slow as your neighbours are
To punish you, may Gorgona shift its ground,

And Capraia, till those islands make a bar
To dam the Arno, and drown your populace –
Every soul in you! Though Ugolino bore

The fame of having betrayed your fortresses,
Still it was wrong in you to so torment
His helpless children.

After love, there is hatred.

In a stunning image, Dante curses Pisa, and imagines moving
the two islands that face one another at the mouth of the Arno to
choke the flow of the river so that it would back up, flood, and
drown every inhabitant.

Hatred of Florence

DANTE ALIGHIERI (1265–1321)

from *The Inferno*
Translated by Gaia Servadio

'The upstart people and the sudden gains,
O Florence, have engendered in thee
pride and excess, so that thou already mourn.'
Thus I spoke with my face uplifted.
The three who understood,
Then looked at one another with the look
Of men who hear the truth.

More on Florence

DANTE ALIGHIERI (1265–1321)

from *The Inferno*

Translated by Gaia Servadio

Godi Fiorenza, poi che se' si grande,
Che per mare e per terra batti l'ali,
E per lo inferno il tuo nome si spande!
Tra li ladron trovai cinque cotali
Tuoi cittadini, onde mi ven vergogna,
e tu in gran orranza non ne sali
Ma se presso al mattin del ver si sogna,
Tu sentirai di qua da picciol tempo
Di quel che Prato, non ch'altri, t'agogna,
E se gia fosse non saria per tempo:
cosi foss'ei, d ache pur esser dee!
Che piu' mi gravera', com' piu' m'attempo.

Florence, rejoice: you have become so great
that you spread your wings over land and sea
And hell rings with your name!
Among the thieves I found five citizens
Of yours, that you honour
And that shames me, you take little honour thus
And yet if dreams we dream at dawn come true
You shall before long feel the weight of what
Prato desires from you, and others as well.
It would, if it had come, not be too soon,
Since come it must, I wish that it had happened,
For it will but hurt me more as I think it over.

Persephone in Spoleto

GAIA SERVADIO

Under a chestnut tree walks Persephone
On a snow-streaked lane.
She came to find her mother's tears.

And then I heard your voice
And dreamt of you
Climbing the hill, joining your hand to mine,
Your hand inside mine
The white cathedral enveloped in swallows.
We looked, so lost, we watched.

Pray, pray that this minute might not be lost
Pray that you might not lose this sight.

Demeter looked for her daughter
Around the yellow fields
And in the distant woods.

We watched the swallows busying the sky
High and walked along the aqueduct
Whence people fly away for love
Perhaps not hand in hand
And sat at a café sensing the shallowness of our day
Perhaps not the Penguin Café.

Our glances, the rigid words, we mumbled.
And when I looked for you, sweet Kore,
You were no longer there
Over the dark woody Monteluco.
You dozed far away, far away from me.

And I remember all those days and nights
Without you, how could it be
that I was without you?
Love plunged, it was gone
Our eyes no longer lost into the knot
Love plunged from the aqueduct and fell
Breaking its wings
Golden feathers in the wind.

Or was it Kore who plunged
On her swift shiny horse? I should have thanked her
For my liberty, and these woods of Umbria
And this olive groves
that no longer talk of you
And the moon not echoing your face
And the square of Spoleto simmering in music;
the swallows singing your name
and the clouds designing your lips.
I thank the Sun for kissing me
Like you did, with His golden touch.

A poem of love and loss, of memories, even of regret.

A Letter

MICHELANGELO (1475–1564)

I have received it, thanks for your courtesy,
And have read it over about twenty times;
Teeth would do as much good for your nature
As food does for the body when it's been fed.
Since I last saw you, I have also learnt
That Cain was one of your ancestors,
And you have not forsaken his legacy:
For when others gain something, you think you've lost it.
Envious, arrogant, enemies of heaven,
You find your neighbour's charity annoying,
And you are friends only with your own ruin.

Since what the Poet says of Pistoia is true
Bear it in mind, and that's enough; and if you
Speak well of Florence you're trying to fool me.
It is a precious jewel,
Surely, but that's not understood by you,
Since meagre wisdom cannot comprehend it.

This letter from Michelangelo, written in rhyme to a hated recipient, Cino da Pistoia, the poet and jurist, is quite mysterious because it is not known why Michelangelo was so angry. On the other hand he did take offence often and easily, as can be seen from his letters to Vittoria Colonna.

The strength of Michelangelo's feelings embraced Florence, Pistoia and Cino.

Of course when he talks about the Poet, he means Dante.

JOURNEYING THROUGH TUSCAN AND UMBRIAN CITIES

Pisa

GABRIELE D'ANNUNZIO (1863–1938)

from *The Silent Cities*

Translated by Gaia Servadio

O Pisa, O Pisa, for the watery
Melody that renders sweet your slumber
I shall praise you like the one who saw
– forgetting your malaise – the blood of dawn
flowing in your heart, and the flame of the Vespers
and the tearful stars of diamond
and the oblivious filter of the moon.

The Florentine Night

LOUIS CARBONNEL (1858–1938)

Translated by Gualtiero Maldè

Stars that light the Florentine night
Stars that shine in the divine darkness
Where the Arno reflects a pale and cold light
I look at you tremble up above…

What a past reflects within you, distant lights?
Without doubt you dream of the second Athens
That was Florence in the abolished past.

French poets were largely seduced by the Levant and by the tempestuous seas of the North. They tended to treat Italy in prose, although some of Stendhal's prose is poetry.

But here is a voice of astonished joy at discovering Florence. Louis Carbonnel, the painter and poet, wrote *Du Rhône à l'Arno* in 1921. His enthusiasm for Tuscany expressed itself in a single sentence 'Florence is such a gift that one cannot pay for it'.

Stanzas

LORD BYRON (1788–1824)

written in passing the Ambracian Gulph

Florence! whom I shall love as well
As ever yet was said or sung
(Since Orpheus sang his spouse from hell)
Whilst thou art fair and I am young;

Sweet Florence! those were pleasant times,
Her worlds were staked for ladies'eyes;
Had bards as many realms as rhymes,
Thy charms might raise new Anthonies.

Though Fate forbids such things to be,
Yet, by thine eyes and ringlets curl'd!
I cannot lose a world for thee,
But would not lose thee for a world.

December in Florence

JOSEPH BRODSKY (1940–96)

I

The doors take in air, exhale steam; you, however, won't
be back to the shallowed Arno where, like a new kind
of quadruped, idle couples follow the river bend.
Doors bang, beasts hit the slabs. Indeed,
the atmosphere of this city retains a bit
of the dark forest. It
is a beautiful city where at certain age
one simply raises the collar to disengage
from passing humans and dulls the gaze.

II

Sunk in raw twilight, the pupil blinks but gulps
the memory-numbing pills of opaque streetlamps.
Yards from where the Signoria looms,
the doorway, centuries later, suggests the best
cause of expulsion; one can't exist
by a volcano and show no fist,
Though it won't unclench when its owner dies.
For death is always a second Florence in terms of size
and its architecture of Paradise.

III

Cats check at noon under benches to see if the shadows are
black, while the old bridge (new after repair),
where Cellini is peering at the hills' blue glare,

buzzes with heavy trading in bric-à-brac.
Flotsam is combed by the arching brick.
And the passing beauty's loose golden lock,
as she rummages through the hawker's herd,
flares up suddenly under the arcade
like an angelic vestige in the kingdom of the dark-haired.

IV

A man gets reduced to pen's rustle on paper, to
wedges, ringlets of letters, and also, due
to the slippery surface, to commas and full stops. True,
often, in some common word, the unwitting pen
strays into drawing – while tackling an
'M' — some eyebrows; ink is more honest than
blood. And a face, with moist words inside
out to dry what has just being said,
smirks like the crumpled paper absorbed by shade.

V

Quays resemble stalled trains. The damp
yellow palazzi are sunk in the earth waist-down.
A shape in an overcoat braves the dank
mouth of a gateway, mounts the decrepit, flat,
worn-out teeth towards their red, inflamed,
palate with its sure-as-fate
number 16. Voiceless, instilling fright,
a little bell in the end prompts a rasping 'Wait!'
Two old crones let you in, each looks like the figure 8.

VI

In a dusty café, in the shade of your cap,
eyes pick out frescoes, nymphs, cupids on their way up.
In a cage, making up for the sour terza-rima crop,
a seedy goldfish juggles his sharp cadenza.
A chance ray of sunlight splattering the palazzo
and the sacristy where lies Lorenzo
pierces thick blinds and titillates the veinous
filthy marble, tubs of snow-white verbena;
and the bird's ablaze within his wire Ravenna.

VII

Taking in air, exhaling steam, the doors
slam shut in Florence. One or two lives one yearns
for (it is up to that faith of yours) –
some night in the first one you learn that love
doesn't move the stars (or the moon) enough.
For it divides things in two, in half.
Like the cash in your dreams. Like your idle fears
of dying. If love were to shift the gears
of the southern stars, they'd run to the virgin spheres.

VIII

The stone nest resounds with a piercing squeal
of brakes. Intersections scare your skull
like crossed bones. In the low December sky
the gigantic egg laid there by Brunelleschi
jerks a tear from an eye experienced in the blessed

domes. A traffic policeman briskly
throws his hand in the air like a letter X.
Loudspeakers bark about rising tax.
Oh, the obvious leaving that 'living' masks!

IX

There are cities one won't see again. The sun
throws its gold at their frozen windows. But all the same
there is no entry, no proper sum.
There are always six bridges spanning the sluggish river.
There are places where lips touched lips for the first time ever
or pen pressed paper with real fervour.
There are arcades, colonnades, ironed idles that blur your lens.
There the streetcar's multitudes, jostling, dense
speak in the tongue of a man who departed thence.

I met Joseph Brodsky (1940-1996) sometime around March
1969 in a flat in the outskirts of Leningrad. People would gather,
each bringing a bottle of vodka or something to eat. They were
all young, all dissident, all writers, and the rooms were small,
poor. I had already read some of Brodsky's poetry and admired
him but since I was accompanied by a kind of Raskolnikov who
was a KGB informer – I didn't know it – he kept to himself.

I saw him again after he had become a Nobel laureate in 1987;
he delivered a talk at the speed of light, even faster than Isaiah
Berlin who indeed confessed that he had missed a great deal of it.

Brodsky was amazed and in a certain sense surprised by the
beauty of Italy; he married a beautiful Venetian woman and
Venice reminded him of his native Leningrad/St Petersburg.

Gianni Schicchi

GIOVACCHINO FORZANO (1884–1970)

Translated by Gaia Servadio

Florence is like a tree in bloom
that has trunk and leaves in Piazza dei Signori,
but its roots bring new strength
from fresh and fecund valleys;
And Florence flourishes
with solid palaces and elegant towers that reach the stars!
The Arno sings before floating into the sea
embracing Piazza Santa Croce,
and its song is so sweet and so sonorous
that a chorus of rivulets tumble down to join it.
Similarly may the academics in arts and science
descend on Florence to make it richer and more splendid.
And from Val d'Elsa below the castles
may well come Arnolfo (di Cambio) to make the tower beautiful
and may Giotto arrive from the wooded Mugello
and the brave Medici merchant!
Enough with mean hatreds and with ripicchi
long live the new people and Gianni Schicchi!

The librettist was the nineteenth-century Italian equivalent of
the screenplay writer of early Hollywood or Cinecitta'. At that
time the Italians did not produce novels, apart from rare
examples like Manzoni's *The Betrothed*. That was because there
was practically no productive middle-class willing to be
entertained by reading. And censorship was ferocious. They had
opera instead. To express thoughts in music – think of

revolutionary Verdi and also Rossini – was safer, and opera reached everybody. It was the most popular form of communication.

While the French and the English produced wonderful novels, Italy built a set of rules around opera; rites and regulations which we still observe today with delight. It is unfashionable to say that the libretti are fine pieces of literature, but some of them are. Some libretti by Piave, Ferretti, Mosca, Giacosa and Illica, da Ponte etc. are works of art.

Puccini was notorious for tormenting his librettists. This famous piece from Puccini's opera *Gianni Schicchi* is by Giovacchino Forzano (who, in turn, took the story from *Il Decamerone* by Boccaccio). We also find Gianni Schicchi in Dante's *Hell* (Canto XXX) ('E l'Aretin, che rimase tremando,/ mi disse 'Quel folletto e' Gianni Schicchi/ e va rabbioso altrui cosi' conciando'). The action takes place in Florence in 1299.

By the River Arno

LORD BRYON (1788–1824)

from *Childe Harold's Pilgrimage (Canto IV)*

XLVIII

But Arno wins us to the fair white walls,
Where the Etrurian Athens claims and keeps
A softer feeling for her fairy halls.
Girt by her theatre of hills, she reaps
Her corn, and wine, and oil, and plenty leaps
To laughing life, with her redundant horn.
Along the bank where smiling Arno sweeps
Was modern Luxury of Commerce born,
And buried learning rose, redeem'd to a new morn.

XLIX

There too the Goddess loves in stone, and fills
The air around with beauty; we inhale
The ambrosial aspect, which, beheld, instils
Part of its immorality; the veil
Of heaven is half undrawn; within the pale
We stand and in that form and face behold
What mind can make, when Nature's self would fail;
And to the fond idolaters of old
Envy the innate flash which such a soul could mould.

A JOURNEY OF MEMORIES AND RECOLLECTIONS

After the War, in Florence
GAIA SERVADIO

One only bridge the SS spared
on the muddy Arno,
that was Pontevecchio.
The heaps of dusty bricks and stones,
the cracked white marbles
strangled our steps.

My mother looked at the silk shirts
Not for us.
The grey stones of Florence blocked the way.

Papà took us to see Michelangelo's Prigioni
sliding in pain from their emprisoned stone.
On the other side of the Arno,
at Camillo's the sage-scented food blessed
Via Santo Spirito. Not for us.
We pressed our faces against the warm windows
And looked at those who ate steaks
and sipped Chianti.

That was the time when my uncle came on a jeep,
He had fled intolerance but lost his dignity.
We people of the war had looked at hunger in its eyes
Envying the corpses that felt no fear
that felt no hunger. We, casualty of disaster,
were alive in Florence. Why were we alive?
Why were we in Florence?

My mother's coat hid her shredded clothes
My sister's shoes in ruins,
the ruins of war had settled
over my father's lost smile.
Memories of his lost smile.

One day the bridges would once more embrace the city
and I would buy a silken shirt for my mother.
One day Florence would lose its dust
and I would smile again, a casualty of war
burying my bitterness under my own ruins.

The Tiny Ant

LORENZO DE' MEDICI (1449–92)

Translated by Ted Hughes

> . . . the tiny ant
> brings the sun's flame, burning and clear,
> out of the ancient caves.
> The sage, who learns instantly
> then tells the others
> where the mean peasant cunningly hid
> a small mound of grain.
> So out hurries the black, possessive horde,
> one by one.
> They come to the pile, and they go.
> They carry the plundered bounty
> in mouths and in hands,
> they arrive eager and light,
> heavy and loaded they go.
> They block the narrow path,
> and collide.

I think it was around 1990 that I asked Ted Hughes to take part in a programme of Italian poetry I was putting together at the Accademia Italiana. I was trying to couple a great Italian poet with a contemporary British poet who could interpret the original. I was lucky, Stephen Spender interpreted Dante Alighieri; Al Alvarez, Primo Levi; Grey Gowrie, Montale; Robert Lowell also Dante and Montale. When it came to Lorenzo il Magnifico, Ted Hughes – whom I had never met – was the ideal poet since he was working on the Renaissance and because he had a natural ear and a vast gammut of inspiration. Amazingly, for me, he accepted (thanks to his wife Carol to whom I am forever grateful). He discarded – rightly – the existing translations and asked me to render the poems of my choice with a literal translation, word by word, on which he then worked. He always grasped the little nuances, the bawdy voice, the desperate woman in love – there was in Ted Hughes both the rare modesty of greatness and the innocence of the poet.

Carnival: A Ballad

LORENZO DE' MEDICI (1449–92)

Translated by Ted Hughes

Alas, during this carnival
we women have mislaid
the six husbands we had.
Without them, things look bad.

We all come from Arcetri.
We work in the orchards there,
we grow a peculiar
fruit fine as our country.

O give a kindly thought –
bring us to our men.
These fruits will be yours, then.
They are sweet, they do not hurt.

We have huge cucumbers –
their skins seem to be studded –
just like warts, all rough and odd,
but they are hearty and wholesome.

You can take them in both hands.
Peel aside a bit of rind,
open your mouth and then suck hard –
you'll soon find it does not hurt.

A watermelon too, as fat
as a pumpkin, among others.
We keep these for the seed

so more can be born
to make the tongue blood-red.
Wings on its feet, like a dragon
fierce and beautiful to look at,
scary, but it cannot hurt.

And look we have long beans
for the gourmet, so tender.
Also these that are bent
hard and big, and good cooked hot
with oil, inside a roll,
you hold on to the bottom
and ply up and down with it –
it threatens, but can't hurt.

They say these fruits of ours
should be eaten after dinner.
To us, that sounds mad.
To digest them is tough.
A body full of dinner
we call full enough.
And yet, before or after, do
just as you please, it's up to you.
But try them before, they're not at all bad.

These fruits that are so good –
if you point out our husbands –
they're yours and free for all.
You see we're fresh and young.
If you've no gratitude
we'll find some other ready hand
to help us plough our bit of land
here at carnival.

A Ballad

LORENZO DE' MEDICI (1449–92)

Translated by Ted Hughes

So what is that man there, with ruddy cheeks,
and two together with him in long cloaks?
And he: 'These three are grave ecclesiastics.

The fattest is the rector of Antella
and so that all might think how well he looks
he always keeps cosmetics in his wallet.

That other, whose sweet laughter you hear ripple,
the one with the pointed nose, long and strange,
has likewise made himself quite comfortable –

his dignity, as Priest of Fiesole,
being also devoted to the cup
which Sir Antonio, his curate, fills

in every corner and at every season
always that loyal vessel's close to hand.
I say no more, before the procession.

But I think he was always his escort.
When he shifts town for town, and court for court,
this is the one who taps upon his door.

So this will be there beside him after his death
and should be placed beside him in his tomb
to comfort both his carcase and his wrath.

This will be his bequest. Have you seen
when, during the procession, a command
brings them all to a halt? And how then,

when his brothers, at the superior's call,
make their circle together, have you seen,
while their lifted cassocks undo them all

how he covers his face – with his cup?

A JOURNEY AROUND DANTE AND THE
BEAUTY OF THE TUSCAN LANGUAGE

The City of Fire

DANTE ALIGHIERI (1265–1321)

Translated by Robert Pinsky

> . . . Oh Tuscan
> who travels alive through this city of fire
> speaking in so elegant a fashion
> if it should please you, stop a moment.
> Your way of speaking shows that you were born
> In the same noble country where
> I possibly have wrought too much harm.

In Dante's journey through hell, purgatory and paradise, in which he talks with the voice of friends and foe, the beauty of the Tuscan language, which he himself uses so beautifully, is celebrated. In hell Farinata degli Uberti, a relative of Guido Cavalcanti, hears Dante's accent and recognizes the harmonious sound.

Many lines from Dante's *Divine Comedy* are printed in my mind and I use them as indeed my father did. He could cite verse after verse, like the English do Shakespeare, at times making fun of us children, at others pinpointing how Dante's vision was still topical and true; nobody expresses thoughts with such precision.

Dante

ANNA AKHMATOVA (1889–1966)

Translated by Irina Zhetesnova

Even after his death he did not return
To the city that nursed him.
Going away, this man did not look back.
To him I sing this song,
Torches, night, a last embrace,
Outside in her streets the mob howling.
He sent her a curse from hell
And in heaven could not forget her.
But never, in a penitent's shirt,
Did he walk barefoot with lighted candle
Through his beloved Florence,
Perfidious, base, and irremediably home.

Anna Akhmatova (1889–1966) wrote this famous sonnet about Dante, and Joseph Brodsky – who translated himself – also laments the fact that 'lo maggior poeta' is buried in Ravenna, far from his native Florence, a cry that echoes an earlier one of Byron's.

Brodsky, Akhmatova and also Byron, each in their own way, knew the pangs of exile.

Ungrateful Florence!

LORD BYRON (1788–1824)

from *Childe Harold's Pilgrimage (Canto IV)*

LVII

Ungrateful Florence! Dante sleeps afar,
Like Scipio, buried by the upbraiding shore;
Thy factions, in their worse than civil war,
Proscribed the bard whose name for evermore
Their children's children would in vain adore
With the remorse of ages; and the crown
Which Petrarch's laureate brow supremely wore,
Upon a far and foreign soil had grown,
His life, his fame, his grave, though rifled – not thine own.

Siren Tongue

LORD BYRON (1788–1824)

from *Childe Harold's Pilgrimage (Canto IV)*

LVIII

Boccaccio to his parent earth bequeathed
His dust – and lies it not her great among,
With many a sweet and solemn requiem breath'd
O'er him who form'd the Tuscan's siren tongue?
That music in itself, whose sounds are song,
The poetry of speech? No – even his tomb
Uptorn, must bear the hyaena bigot's wrong,
No more admist the meaner dead find room,
Nor claim a passing sigh, because it told for whom!

A JOURNEY AROUND MYSELF

An Ego Trip

I should have introduced myself at the beginning, before starting this compilation because I am the author of three poems which I have immodestly included. One of them was originally written in Italian and I later translated it into English.

My connection with Umbria and Tuscany derives from the fact that I live in Umbria (between Todi and Spoleto) and that I have an addiction to Tuscan literature and people. I adore the Tuscan accent and their choice of words; the Florentines are masters of inventive maledictions and the unfortunate Holy Mother is often the target of hilarious witticisms. When I am in Siena, where the very finest Italian is spoken, I ask the way just to hear the Sienese speak. I am often in Florence where I have good friends, good food and good opera at the Comunale.

I know both regions well but my roots are elsewhere.

I am partly Roman and Sicilian (of Norman stock) on my mother's side; from Turin and Ancona on my father's, hence I am a true Italian, alien to the *campanilismo*, the parochialism that affects most Italians and for which points are scored by one city against another. On the other hand one of the miracles of Italy rests precisely on the diversity of its territory: one crosses the Apennines from Emilia and the landscape changes, the architecture is different, the cuisine is diverse and so are the ingredients. Even the olive tree is pruned in different ways from region to region, from hillside to hillside, and, naturally, each *contadino* proclaims that his method is the best.

In spite of being a native, I am always stunned by the beauty of my country and also by a deeply-digested culture more present, now as in times gone by, within the simple people than in the fat middle-class: 'I subiti guadagni'. New money, as Dante infers on page 71.

My early life echoes with poetry – Homer, Leopardi and Dante reigned supreme in my house. A *versetto* from 'L'Infinito' marks my mother's tomb today and the final line of Dante's *Commedia*, so beloved by my father, are on the slab of stone which covers his body.

> *L'amor che move il sole e l'altre stelle.*

Poetry came first for me, before prose, as I could hear it being recited before I could read – I was quite a slow reader, in all senses. I myself wrote poetry since I can remember; an early one was about hearing my parents' voices playing bridge – quarrelling, of course – and keeping us children awake. At school we were made to learn by heart whole cantos by Homer, by Dante even Victor Hugo, in translation, not to mention Manzoni who I hated.

Mary MacCarthy used to mumble lines of poetry often. She used to tell me that were she made a political prisoner and forced to spend years in prison, she would have many poems to tell herself and that that was why she kept them alive in her memory.

An anthology of poetry like this means making a few sacrifices. For example I have snubbed Poliziano, the gentle teacher of Lorenzo de Medici – the Botticelli of poetry – but I would not have been able to render the music of his ballads; I sacrificed Compiuta Donzella, a Florentine poetess (second half of the thirteenth century) who laments her fate: her tyrant father wanted her to marry a man she abhorred. In the *Aeneid*, a more mature Virgil, more mature than in the *Georgics* that is, describes how the Etruscans rally to the side of Aeneas to fight the horrible tyrant – an improbable political situation.

In some cases I have kept the original, at times I have been lucky with the translations; but poetry, as we all know, is untranslatable. *Traduttore, traditore,* we say. All the same, evocative words make one dream and what is better than a dream?

I end as I should end, with Lorenzo's sonnet about death.

Death

LORENZO DE' MEDICI (1449–92)

Translated by Ted Hughes

How futile every hope is, that we have,
how illusory, all our designs,
and how crammed this world with ignorance,
we learn from our master – the Grave.

Some think singing and dancing and parties are life,
some let quieter matters guide their minds,
some detest the world and its substance,
some live a secret they show nothing of.

Vain worries and thoughts, and diverse fates
for the whole variety of creation,
find us, each time, straying over the earth.

Each thing has a moment that flits,
for Fortune's a sickness of perpetual motion.
Nothing is still. And nothing lasts. Only death.

ACKNOWLEDGEMENTS

My thanks go to Alexandra de Leal for labouring on my behalf;
likewise Professor Luca Pietromarchi of the Roma 3 University;
Carol Hughes for allowing me to use her husband's translations
of Lorenzo de' Medici and Hugh Myddelton Biddulph for his
English vocabulary.

The publishers would like to thank the following publishers for
permission to quote from their titles:
Alistair Elliot for permission to use his translations of Dante's
'Inferno, XXIV' and of Carducci's 'The Sources of Clitumnus',
from *Italian Landscape Poems*, edited by Alistair Elliot; Farrar
Straus & Giroux for permission to use Robert Lowell's trans-
lation of Eugenio Montale's 'News from Monte Amiata', from
Lowell's collection of loose translations of European poets,
Imitations, for permission to use an extract from Robert Pinsky's
translation of Dante's 'Inferno', and for permission to use
'December in Florence' by Joseph Brodsky.

INDEX OF POETS

INDEX OF TRANSLATORS

INDEX OF FIRST LINES

I have received it, thanks for your courtesy 76
I knew all too well that one cannot 69
I love you, city of quarrels, angry Pistoia 57
In Santa Croce's holy precincts lie 55
In the orchard, at Massa – Oh! azure blocks 41

Leonardo da Vinci, deep and dark mirror 54
Less and less fearful, more and more beautiful 66

Montefalco.You were frescoed by Benozzo 50
Most high, all powerful, good Lord! 39

O Pisa, O Pisa, for the watery 79
. . . Oh Tuscan who travels alive through this city 103
One only bridge the SS spared 93

. . . Pistoia in parte rebellar vedevi 53

Since I do not hope to go back ever 63
So what is that man there, with ruddy cheeks 99
Stabat mater dolorosa 42
Stars that light the Florentine night 81

The doors take in air, exhale steam; you, however 83
The little brooks which down from the green hills 23
The sun is set; the swallows are asleep 32
. . . the tiny ant brings the sun's flame, burning 95
'The upstart people and the sudden gains, 71
They make no noise, though their wings move 30

Under a chestnut tree walks Persephone 74
Ungrateful Florence! Dante sleeps afar 105

You saw how Pistoia rebelled, in part 52